D0765538

URBAN
SURVIVAL TECHNIQUES

ELITE FORCES SURVIVAL GUIDE SERIES

Elite Survival

Survive in the Desert with the French Foreign Legion

Survive in the Arctic with the Royal Marine Commandos

Survive in the Mountains with the U.S. Rangers and Army
  Mountain Division

Survive in the Jungle with the Special Forces "Green Berets"

Survive in the Wilderness with the Canadian and Australian
  Special Forces

Survive at Sea with the U.S. Navy SEALs

Training to Fight with the Parachute Regiment

The World's Best Soldiers

Elite Operations and Training

Escape and Evasion

Surviving Captivity with the U.S. Air Force

Hostage Rescue with the SAS

How to Pass Elite Forces Selection

Learning Mental Endurance with the U.S. Marines

Special Forces Survival Guidebooks

Survival Equipment

Navigation and Signaling

Surviving Natural Disasters

Using Ropes and Knots

Survival First Aid

Trapping, Fishing, and Plant Food

Urban Survival Techniques

URBAN
SURVIVAL TECHNIQUES

PATRICK WILSON

**Introduction by Colonel John T. Carney. Jr., USAF–Ret.
President, Special Operations Warrior Foundation**

MASON CREST PUBLISHERS

This edition first published in 2003
by Mason Crest Publishers Inc.
370 Reed Road, Broomall, PA, 19008

Library of Congress Cataloging-in-Publication Data available

ISBN 1-59084-020-8

Editorial and design by
Amber Books Ltd.
Bradley's Close
74–77 White Lion Street
London N1 9PF

Project Editor Chris Stone
Designer Simon Thompson
Picture Research Lisa Wren

Printed and bound in Malaysia

10 9 8 7 6 5 4 3 2 1

ACKNOWLEDGMENT
For authenticating this book, the Publishers would like to thank the Public Affairs Offices of the U.S. Special Operations Command, MacDill AFB, FL.; Army Special Operations Command, Fort Bragg, N.C.; Navy Special Warfare Command, Coronado, CA.; and the Air Force Special Operations Command, Hurlbert Field, FL.

IMPORTANT NOTICE
The survival techniques and information described in this publication are for use in dire circumstances where the safety of the individual is at risk. Accordingly, the publisher cannot accept any responsibility for any prosecution or proceedings brought or instituted against any person or body as a result of the uses or misuses of the techniques and information within.

DEDICATION
This book is dedicated to those who perished in the terrorist attacks of September 11, 2001, and to the Special Forces soldiers who continually serve to defend freedom.

Picture Credits
Corbis: 17, 24, 26, 32, 36; **Military Picture Library**: 6, 19; **TRH**: 8, 10, 12, 28, 30, 34, 38, 40, 56 Ilustrations courtesy of Amber Books and the following supplied by Patrick Mulrey: 13, 15, 20, 22, 35, 42, 43, 45, 46, 47, 48, 50, 52, 53, 54
Front Cover: **Corbis** (inset); **TRH/P. Valpolini** (main)

CONTENTS

INTRODUCTION

Elite forces are the tip of Freedom's spear. These small, special units are universally the first to engage, whether on reconnaissance missions into denied territory for larger, conventional forces or in direct action, surgical operations, preemptive strikes, retaliatory action, and hostage rescues. They lead the way in today's war on terrorism, the war on drugs, the war on transnational unrest, and in humanitarian operations as well as nation building. When large scale warfare erupts, they offer theater commanders a wide variety of unique, unconventional options.

Most such units are regionally oriented, acclimated to the culture and conversant in the languages of the areas where they operate. Since they deploy to those areas regularly, often for combined training exercises with indigenous forces, these elite units also serve as peacetime "global scouts" and "diplomacy multipliers," a beacon of hope for the democratic aspirations of oppressed peoples all over the globe.

Elite forces are truly "quiet professionals": their actions speak louder than words. They are self-motivated, self-confident, versatile, seasoned, mature individuals who rely on teamwork more than daring-do. Unfortunately, theirs is dangerous work. Since "Desert One"—the 1980 attempt to rescue hostages from the U.S. embassy in Tehran, for instance—American special operations forces have suffered casualties in real world operations at close to fifteen times the rate of U.S. conventional forces. By the very nature of the challenges which face special operations forces, training for these elite units has proven even more hazardous.

Thus it's with special pride that I join you in saluting the brave men and women who volunteer to serve in and support these magnificent units and who face such difficult challenges ahead.

Colonel John T. Carney, Jr., USAF–Ret.
President, Special Operations Warrior Foundation

Soviet Spetsnaz soldiers train in real-life situations. Bending the shoulder back in this direction can be very painful for an assailant.

WHAT IS SELF-DEFENSE?

For the world's elite forces, training the mind to work out dangerous situations accurately, to avoid fights, and to stay alert and positive is vital to successful self-defense. This positive mental outlook, combined with a knowledge of self-defense techniques, reduces the risk of being attacked and becoming a victim.

In this book, you will learn some of the elite troops' combat techniques, including speed and aggression, though not the **lethal** moves that are used in combat. In training, troops are taught to be ruthless—the faster the fight is over, the better. The British **SAS**, for example, aim for the "five-second knockdown," overcoming their **adversary** in less than five seconds.

Self-defense does not just involve learning techniques—far from it. It begins with a positive mental outlook and a few simple precautions, which will let troops anticipate and avoid potential trouble. This knowledge will also enable you to deal with trouble when it occurs.

Around 90 percent of successful self-defense has to do with avoiding violence. The remaining 10 percent depends on using physical action to combat the attacker. Getting into a fight is easy. Avoiding a fight is the difficult part, but to do that successfully, troops have to be aware of all the situations and circumstances in which trouble is likely to arise.

U.S. Rangers practice luring an opponent into believing the captured soldier is totally submissive before launching a counterattack.

Fighting technique is essential, but so too is physical strength and endurance. U.S. Marines are put through rigorous fitness regimes to improve their stamina and maximize their fighting strength.

The response

To be effective, troops make sure they are fit and that they are trained in self-defense. Increased fitness and physical skills boost their self-confidence and help them to think clearly and quickly, to stay aware of potential dangers, and to focus their energies if the time comes for physical action. Good self-defense is about being prepared and having the knowledge to overcome challenges.

When to use self-defense

All people have the right to defend themselves against physical attack. If elite soldiers have done everything in their power to avoid conflict, and there is no chance of getting away, then they have to commit fully to the fight. Knowledge, skill, and the conviction of your moral right will give you the determination and power to win. Some of the most ferocious fighters in both the animal and the human worlds are mothers with young children. They do not even have to think about the rights and wrongs of their actions; they just do what has to be done to protect their young.

To summarize, self-defense is the art of avoiding trouble. Troops have to know and recognize the dangers, but when, despite their best efforts, conflict is inevitable, they must know what to do. Their minds and bodies must be prepared to carry out the moves they have practiced. Surprise and strong action, combined with a strong mental attitude and a sense that they are in the right, should see them through.

Discipline

The majority of people who cause trouble are not trained and do not know how to fight. So, the first thing that elite soldiers are taught in training is discipline. They have to learn to control their movements and the emotions that can go with them. They will learn how to strike blows, but also never to strike them in anger. The code of honor, which governs the best **martial arts** organizations, goes beyond the training rooms into everyday life.

This is the opposite of the behavior of the undisciplined street fighters. They have no training, no discipline, and are not really that accomplished at what they do. Most of the people acting aggressively in the street are bullies. They can charge forward, swinging

U.S. troops learning to throw and break falls. Military clothing, being strongly made, makes it ideal for executing throws.

when they are under the influence of alcohol or narcotics, but their timing is erratic and they have only false courage.

Respecting personal space

Troops learn that they can often avoid trouble by taking care not to invade someone's space. They watch where they are walking. They do not get too close to someone they are walking behind.

They do not crowd people. It makes those people nervous and could trigger violence. They avoid the bully's clumsy attempts to get them into a fight.

Ready to defend himself. The body position elite troops are trained to adopt if threatened.

Levels of alertness

Troops think about alertness as a series of levels, through which they move up and down like a driver changing gears according to traffic and road conditions.

Level One

When they are at home, or in barracks, they are safe. They know where everything is and they are at their most relaxed. This level of alertness is known as Level One.

The moment soldiers leave the safety of the barracks, they must be prepared to move up to the next level of alertness.

Level Two

At this level of alertness, and having left the safety of "home," soldiers need to be fully aware of their immediate environment. They assess the world around them with scanning glances. First they look up, then to the left and right, but in a fairly relaxed way. This should not be a nervous reaction. This sort of alertness becomes second nature to people who spend a lot of time out in the wilderness, in woods, and on mountains. By paying attention, they avoid tripping over rocks and treading on snakes. In addition, they see animal tracks and recognize birds and small creatures, information that can be extremely useful to them if they are in a survival situation and looking for food.

In the urban environment, Level Two alertness indicates the first stage of self-defense. Soldiers will look over their shoulders now and then, look up at buildings and trees, and check in front of them at all times. They will ask themselves questions such as, "Why is that man standing on the street corner?" or "Am I in danger of being attacked in this situation?"

This approach is essential in cases of urban unrest, such as anti-government or **anarchist** demonstrations. Armies are often called to assist the police with riot control. In these situations, soldiers must be able to recognize the point at which peaceful protest might spill over into violence. This is often a thin line, and elite soldiers will do well to remember their training.

Level Three

If soldiers notice something unusual, Level Three alertness must automatically take over. Level Three focuses all their attention on the task in hand, and prepares them for combat if other, more peaceable techniques fail.

If soldiers believe the situation needs to be avoided or it is dangerous to them, they will head for a gathering of people, where there is a good chance of getting help. (If soldiers are in a non-urban environment, such as jungle, they will attempt to conceal themselves until the danger passes.) If the situation does not let them seek out safety in numbers, and they are trapped with someone who is approaching them aggressively, self-defense is often the only option. Now is the time to think and act logically.

Note the body language in this picture. The soldier on the right is being much more aggressive by touching his adversary. His opponent shows restraint but is still in an excellent position to attack if needed.

Confrontation

The easiest way to get into a confrontation is to be drawn into a verbal disagreement. Often this can happen as a result of getting involved in a **macho** staring game. Soldiers are taught not to stare back. If they are challenged in this sort of situation, they avoid giving any "smart" answers. Instead, they try to be friendly and try to demonstrate they have no aggressive intentions. If the other person continues to be aggressive, then the soldier knows that he wants to fight.

The rules of confrontation are useful in a **captivity** situation. If soldiers have been caught behind enemy lines and have been taken away for **interrogation**, the last thing they want to do is further **antagonize** their captors with unfriendly behavior.

Dialogue

Troops are trained to approach confrontation using a technique known as the "two D" rule. The first "D" is Dialogue. When the aggressor makes a verbal challenge, the soldier responds in a peaceful and friendly manner.

Direction

The next "D" is Direction. If the aggressor continues to approach, members of the elite forces say, "Stop! Hold it!" They put up their hands at chest level, with the palms open and facing outward. This means soldiers are issuing a passive, spoken warning. Soldiers speak in a loud voice, to draw other people's attention to what is happening. They want others to witness their secondary

Troops in the Vietnamese 47th Regiment practice martial arts self-defense during training in Hanoi, 1991.

instructions: "Drop the knife! Don't come any nearer!" These statements indicate the Direction technique, and witnesses will have taken note of what is happening.

The soldiers have tried to **defuse** the situation with simple words, and have progressed to a very firm and unmistakable verbal warning. If the aggressor makes a grab for them at this point, they are entitled to do everything in their power to stop the attack. However, they cannot let the aggressor come too close before they act. Whoever throws the first punch is likely to be the winner.

THE SAS AND SELF-DEFENSE

The characteristics of military close-combat situations, feature a level of violence which is inappropriate in a civilian setting. Members of the British SAS are taught what are known as "speed kills." The fastest draw, or the fastest punch or strike, is the one that keeps them alive and results in their enemy being dead or injured. In Close Quarter Battle (CQB), troops use anything that comes to hand, and they move with explosive speed and aggression. The intensity of elite soldiers' attack or counterattack must be such a surprise that their opponents have no time to respond. In CQBs, if soldiers do not have a real or improvised weapon, they use their bodies' weapons. In the military context, different rules apply because the opponent is a true enemy. He has to be neutralized.

Troops are trained to issue clear, firm verbal commands. Most people have been exposed to some form of discipline at some time and, like a dog conditioned to its master's commands, the attacker will hesitate, even if it is only for a fraction of a second. His discipline and reactions may be slower than the elite forces soldiers', but in the back of his mind the command registers, and he knows that he is in the wrong. He may well keep coming, but the soldiers know that they have weakened their attacker's self-confidence, and they now have time to make the first strike.

Spetsnaz soldiers are unarmed combat specialists. They take training to the extreme. Kicking an opponent is preferable to close-quarter combat because soldiers can see what they are doing more clearly.

During riot control, it is imperative that elite troops keep their discipline in the face of taunting and confrontational gestures.

Body language

Academic research has shown that we communicate far more information through physical means, such as facial expressions, **posture**, movements and **gestures**, than through language. In fact, what we say is usually confirmed by our body language.

Much of the time, we are not even aware of the information we are absorbing and processing from someone else's body language, choice of clothing and hairstyle, and overall behavior.

On the battlefield, the usual place a soldier engages in combat, body language plays less part in the proceedings. Troops fire at a "faceless" enemy in an **indiscriminate** way, never getting close enough to see the reaction of their enemy. But in one-on-one combat situations, which tend to arise in urban environments, soldiers must note the actions of their opponents to gain insight into their mood and likely response.

Signals

In self-defense situations, both the aggressor and potential victim use their knowledge of body language. Someone who has a timid posture and creeps along the street looking fearful appears to be an easier target than someone walking confidently, with the head held high. Aggressors depend a lot on body language, because their aim

THE EYES AND CHARACTER

Eyes can sometimes be a clue to character. When an average person is relaxed and not looking up or down, the iris (the colored part of the eye, outside the pupil) contacts the lids at the top and bottom. In some people's eyes, there is a space, with white showing between the bottom of the iris and the bottom lid, and this can indicate a cruel and ambitious nature. The reverse pattern, with white showing between the top lid and the top of the iris, can indicate an aggressive nature. This is sometimes referred to as "mad, staring eyes." If someone has eyes with white showing all around the iris, it is possible that they could be in a mentally disturbed state of mind.

Troops training with cudgel sticks; they may look strange, but they are the safest way of training while being protected from serious injury.

is to intimidate. They may puff up their chests, try to make their shoulders look broader. Alternatively, they may roll the sleeves of their T-shirts high to emphasize tightened upper arm muscles. Troops are trained to recognize and interpret these complex signals quickly.

The eyes

The appearance of our eyes and the way we use them can convey a huge amount of information. When you first begin to talk to someone, you make eye contact. Immediately, there is an exchange or information. If they start looking away, it could indicate that they are feeling guilty about something. If they open their eyes very wide when talking to you, they could be trying to **feign** innocence. Some people blink a lot when they are nervous. Others show that they are **intimidated** by avoiding eye contact altogether, or dropping their head forward so that they have to look upward at the person to whom they are talking.

Nonviolent signs

Some people start to groom themselves when they are nervous or upset. They straighten their shirt, adjust their hair, or brush imaginary dirt from the front of their jacket. The man who grooms himself in a dangerous situation is unlikely to get involved in violence. He does not want to end up rolling on the floor getting covered in dirt and blood. Nervous actions such as these are a good indication to the elite soldier that this person poses very little physical threat.

BEING ASSERTIVE AND THE WILL TO WIN

Rolling up the shirt sleeves or removing a jacket is an aggressive gesture. If troops want to calm a dangerous situation, they make all their movements slow when talking to an aggressor. They do not move their shoulders or arms about in the air and they do not crouch in a combat-ready position.

Although soldiers need to retain a nonviolent situation, they cannot afford to let potential opponents think they can do what they want. Bodily contact is strictly prohibited. If the aggressor starts to jab at the soldier with his finger, he is testing to see just how aggressive he can be. He may be trying to provoke the soldier into physical action, but he may also be trying to make the soldier retreat. In this situation, troops use Direction commands such as, "Don't do that. Keep away from me. Don't touch me." These words tell the aggressor that you do not want to hit him. If the aggressor repeats his actions, the soldier will put him down fast and hard.

When troops use Direction commands to control situations they are being **assertive**. They have to be aware of the difference between assertiveness and aggression, and use language accordingly. Troops also remember the Dialogue rules, and give people the option of backing down. They never threaten and never make promises.

Riot police take an assertive stance against an angry mob of protesters in Genoa, Italy, July 20, 2001.

Sometimes troops are tested to their limits by lawlessness, but they must remain calm. These Indonesian students, rioting in 1998, use any weapon they can against the troops.

Maintaining assertiveness

Troops keep their voices down and never lay hands on anyone (unless it is a conflict situation). Physical contact with an opponent gives the aggressor the excuse and the motivation to take action. When trying to talk someone out of a confrontation, troops do not adopt an aggressive posture. Standing face-on with their arms folded over their chest may be regarded as aggressive, but it is also tactically weak, since the soldiers would not be able to free their arms fast enough to protect against a punch.

If soldiers are trying to stop someone coming close to them, they must hold their hands at chest level with the palms turned outward. This emphasises their Dialogue commands—"Stay away!"—and their hands are correctly positioned if they are drawn into a fight. The open palms are a good gesture, proving that they have no weapons. Troops remember to be assertive without being threatening.

It is vital that troops control their anger when faced with these situations. It is anger that makes them appear threatening. In any encounter, soldiers always want the other person to underestimate them. If soldiers lose their tempers, then they lose their power. They also lose their coordination, so that they start to fight with their "hearts" instead of their brains. If soldiers get angry, it is likely that all their training will be useless, and they will use only brute force and ignorance. Anger destroys fighting discipline. If opponents are also trained, and have remained cooler, they will beat the soldiers. It is therefore essential for elite troops to give an attacker a false sense of security by staying calm and collected.

Role-playing

Physical self-defense techniques have to be practiced with a partner, and this sort of rehearsal is equally useful with nonphysical techniques. In training, troops take turns being the aggressor and the person under threat. First, they act out what it feels like to be a victim. They use a victim's submissive body language while the aggressor uses threatening body language to invade their personal space, staring them down and using verbal threats. They repeat the

French Foreign Legionnaires practicing hand-to-hand combat. The soldier on the left has succeeded in overpowering his opponent, locking his right arm and forcing an elbow into his face.

exercise, switching roles, and taking turns being assertive, putting up their hands, palms outward, and issuing loud, firm directions, such as, "Stop! Don't do that! Leave me alone!" They learn what it feels like to be both the person issuing the assertive commands and the person receiving them. The more troops practice vocalizing their assertiveness, the easier they find it to use these skills for real.

The will to win

Adopting the correct mental attitude is absolutely essential for successful self-defense. Troops learn to have great self-belief, to read a potential aggressor's body language, and to train their minds to overcome fear. With the right mental approach, they can even deal with the impact of physical pain. For successful self-defense, elite soldiers need to believe in themselves. They also need to have self-esteem, which means respect for themselves. Believing in themselves is partly about having confidence in their ability to deter or overcome an attack. They will have learned self-defense techniques and practiced them repeatedly until they are second nature.

A high degree of self-esteem is vital. In a conflict, this is important because soldiers know that they are in the right. To be prepared for an unexpected attack, they have to get their minds focused. If soldiers are faced by someone who is trying to **violate**, injure, or even kill, they need to alter their mindsets quickly. They must have strong mental attitudes and control their emotions. Confidence, self-belief, and high self-esteem are the keys to success.

Self-defense training is constructed from three basic elements: knowledge, technique, and the will to live. We will examine each of these in turn.

Knowledge

This is the need to understand the way an opponent behaves. It involves a familiarity with the battle terrain and the physical options it provides. Soldiers also need confidence in their own abilities and in their basic army training.

Technique

This is the soldiers' determination, fighting skill, energy, and power in a combat situation. Technique is the foundation of soldiers' training and gives them power to survive in extreme circumstances.

The will to live

Soldiers can have all the knowledge and skill in the world, but without the will to live they could die. It is a natural instinct, but elite troops need to make sure they nourish it. In most situations, an aggressor will also have the will to live and survive. Elite soldiers are therefore taught to be stronger than the aggressor. Only then will they be sure of overcoming and winning the battle.

The will to win is not only a feature of combat. The principle has parallels in other areas of life too. The will to win is the difference between champions and losers in the world of sports and business. The champion has that superior determination and mental ability, as well as essential physical skills. All winners have

A U.S. Marine sergeant prepares a recruit prior to cudgel practice. A soldier's will to win is as important in training as in real-life combat.

This Russian soldier in the Naval Infantry shows excellent balance with a high kick. This would disorientate his opponent, giving the soldier the opportunity to use his AK bayonet to devastating effect.

this quality in common. Some call it having a "big heart" or a "killer instinct." Too many people ignore this important psychological element.

When a fight is about to happen, soldiers must feel 100 percent sure that they are going to win. They build up aggression consciously, and trigger the **adrenaline** rush that helps them win. It does not matter how big the opponent is, or whether he has a baseball bat or a knife. Any nagging doubts troops may have, any fears about their own weaknesses, will let them down. Soldiers use their mental strength to overcome these factors.

OVERCOMING FEAR

Fear is a very natural response to being attacked, and everyone feels it. People who say that they are frightened of nothing are fooling themselves. Members of the British SAS elite forces experience fear just like anyone else. In fact, anyone claiming not to experience fear would never pass the SAS selection process.

Fear is regarded by the elite forces as a positive emotion. However, it is possible to become **immobile** by fear, like a rabbit confronted by a snake, and it is this response that enemy troops seek in their victims. Society's attitude often regards fear as a negative emotion, but the opposite is true. Fear can help fighting troops, as they can control it and use it in their defense.

When you are frightened, the **adrenal glands** release adrenaline into the bloodstream. The effect of this is that, for a short time at least, the body can summon inner reserves of energy and strength. It is the equivalent of a turbo charger in a car. People can run faster and lift heavier weights, and their senses are sharpened—eyesight, hearing, and the senses of smell, touch, and taste. This is a survival mechanism that all animals have, including humans, and it is the basis of the "fight or flight" reaction to stress.

The danger in a combat situation is that troops may lose control of all this useful energy and descend into panic, so they have to learn

Navy SEALs storm a building during training for the Gulf War. The fear-factor is not knowing what they will find behind the door.

To take an enemy by surprise requires daring, speed, and skill. These troops practice for such a moment, using smoke grenades and abseiling ropes. They are wearing S8 respirators to aid breathing.

how to coordinate these emergency powers. This is partly a question of focusing the mind on the task at hand. Most people, including elite soldiers, can perform amazing acts of courage or strength in a tense situation that would otherwise have been beyond them. That is the power of adrenaline. In self-defense situations, soldiers have to perform efficiently using their adrenaline. Focusing, a sense of timing, and basic training—these all come together to help them make the most of their fear.

Learning to "breathe"

One way to exert control over what is happening is to use a breathing technique. Troops inhale through their nose, and concentrate on a point an inch or so (a few centimeters) beneath

Sniper fire is a very real danger in built-up areas. This soldier checks for possible enemy positions, using the wall for protection.

These U.S. Marines practice hand-to-hand fighting under the watchful eye of a combat instructor on board the *USS Kearsarage* in 1991.

their navel for a count of five. They retain the breath for a further five seconds, and then **exhale** through the mouth. They try to repeat the cycle if they have time. This helps them to use their adrenaline reflexes—something they can call upon when faced with a life or death situation. For instance, if a soldier wakes in the night to find her camp on fire, she can use breathing exercises to help her assess the situation and choose the right action instead of panicking.

The reactions of elite troops are super-fast (that is why these troops are the best of the best) and, for them, time seems to slow down. Civilians who have been in a car accident where the car has rolled over have also often described how everything seemed to be in slow motion. In this state of mind, people can see everything coming, including punches and kicks, and have time to avoid them.

By controlling breathing, and focusing on what is happening as the adrenaline flows, elite soldiers can work out what to do next and take action. If they are going into a sequence of strikes, which they have trained for, they focus on where each strike will land. At the same time, soldiers need to remain as relaxed as possible, to avoid their muscles tightening up and becoming too tense. This will only hamper their efforts.

Learning to lose

Many people are reluctant to fight, not only because they do not want to be hurt, but also because they are frightened of losing. However, it is important for soldiers to learn how to lose before they learn how to win. This is where their training comes in. If they are used to simulating fights with training partners, they will gradually lose the fear of defeat that could **paralyze** them in a real-life self-defense situation.

The aggressor on the street may well be bigger and stronger than the soldier. However strong he is, the aggressor lacks discipline. If the soldier has a strong mental attitude, and has conquered his fear of losing by experiencing the reality of combat, the over-confident aggressor is going to be taken aback. Conversely, instead of being intimidated, the elite soldier goes forward and delivers an efficient strike. When attacked, the aggressor will not know what to do, giving the soldier the chance to follow through and complete his fighting sequence.

Coping with pain

All people are understandably frightened of pain, yet pain is natural and useful, and prevents soldiers from damaging their bodies with unwise actions. Pain tells soldiers that something is wrong so that they can do something about it. Without pain, the body would accept damaging burns and wounds. In training, soldiers are trained to understand the function of pain. They can then go on to conquer their fear of it. Pain and fear go together in many ways, and both

"Milling" is a demanding element of British Parachute training. Soldiers must fight toe-to-toe with a fellow recruit for one minute. Recruits must show aggression but, above all, be able to take the pain.

can be overcome. In a fight, when adrenaline is flowing, the body can temporarily **suppress** pain. In combat, people who have suffered broken limbs, been stabbed, and even shot, often do not notice until after the fight. The pain starts only when the adrenaline returns to the adrenal glands. Only then will soldiers become aware of their injuries.

The following summarizes elite soldiers' preparation and training for a physical fight.

• Get the adrenaline flowing when conflict is unavoidable.
• Control the new energy.
• Control the fear of fighting.
• Control the fear of pain.
• Use self-defense techniques.

CONTROLLING FEAR WHEN PARACHUTING

The SAS are trained soldiers and paratroopers, yet even they feel fear when, for instance, they jump out of an airplane. The act itself is frightening and seems to go against natural logic. They do it because they are trained. They know the risks, but they are trained to overcome their fears. Apart from anything else, they are in front of their fellow soldiers, and perhaps even more scared of letting them down. Overcoming the fear and jumping, proves their reliability. All fears can be overcome and controlled, and this applies equally to fighting.

BODY WEAPONS

Troops can use most parts of the body to defend themselves from an attacker. With the proper training and knowledge, troops can call upon their own personal arsenal to beat off and escape from violent assaults.

Sometimes the only weapons troops will have in a self-defense situation will be their hands and arms. When used correctly, these can be extremely effective, letting the soldier defeat an attacker and escape.

The correct stance

If trouble is about to start and soldiers cannot get away quickly, they need to be well-balanced, in order to move easily in any direction. They keep their feet about shoulder's width apart, no more than 18 inches (45 cm). They stand at an oblique angle to the potential attacker—about 30 degrees. This gives them good balance, front and back, as well as to either side.

Soldiers always stand on the balls of their feet so that they have their weight and balance point in the center. They keep their knees slightly bent, their chins down, elbows in to their sides, and their hands up. Elite soldiers will not form a fist, since they have much more flexibility with their hands open.

The U.S. Army soldiers at Ranger training school. *The U.S. Army Hand-to-Hand Combat Manual* forms the basis of their training.

The classic fighting stance: knees slightly bent, chin down, elbows and hands up.

The head

A person's body has many natural weapons. Starting at the top, there is the head. This is a big, bony structure. The hardest part of the skull is the back, while the forehead and bone structure around the face is also fairly strong. If a smaller person is grabbed by someone larger, he or she can use the head as a devastating weapon. Elite soldiers are trained to use their foreheads to butt an aggressor anywhere in the face. If they hit above the eyes, this will probably cause a cut. Although the enemy should be able to see through the blood, many people become alarmed and distracted once they know they are bleeding.

Elite soldiers need to keep their chins tucked in. This is to protect their necks, and to make sure they do not bite their tongues. If they are held in a tight grip and cannot move their arms or knees, the head butt is a good opener to make the attacker let go. It can also be effective if soldiers are grabbed from behind. They can quickly snap their heads back, shoving the hardest part of the head into the enemy's face.

Biting an opponent causes real pain and will make him loosen his hold.

Note: Troops have to remember that the top of the head is a very vulnerable area, and a strike to the **temples** can be extremely dangerous for the victim. A soldier never strikes someone in the temples unless their life is at risk.

Teeth

A soldier's teeth can be a useful weapon in a combat situation. No matter how weak or unfit a person is, a bite can cause an incredible amount of pain if an attacker gets within range. When a dog bites, it does not have that much power; it generates power by clinging to the victim, ripping and tearing at the skin.

Hands and arms

Most people think of using their hands to punch an attacker. However, it can often be more effective to strike with the fingers. If someone attacks an elite soldier, the most effective strike is a jab with the fingers into the aggressor's eyes. An elite soldier goes straight for the eyes and uses all fingers extended in a fast snapping strike. The fingers are to be extended, but not locked straight. There must be a very slight curve in the fingers, so that if the soldier misses and hits bone, the fingers won't break. With all four fingers extended, the soldier's chance of an accurate strike is far improved, and even if he or she gets only one eye, the pain will distract the attacker, and possibly even cause him to lose his balance. This will not necessarily win the fight immediately, but it will weaken the attacker. A soldier's fingers are also essential for applying disabling locks to the attacker's wrists and fingers.

Palm strikes

The hand is also used for striking, and troops are trained to use the palm of the hand. If an attacker is in front, the elite soldier can step forward and strike with the heel of the palm up into his chin. It takes a lot less skill than a punch, it will not damage the hand, and can be much more damaging. It is best if combined with an earlier distraction strike—ideally the fingers to the eyes as described above. It is not a jab; it is a full-blooded strike. The soldier will come in toward his opponent as he hits, and follow through past the point of impact. He drives the palm up into the chin—and if he misses, he can continue the move into the nose.

Punches

The first thing for soldiers to do if they are going to punch is to form the fist properly. They must curl their fingers in tightly against the palm, and tuck the thumb down the outside, across the index and middle fingers. When soldiers throw a punch, they need to straighten up the bones and muscles in the arm. They will twist the arm as they throw the punch, so that they hit with the palm down. The top knuckles should be in line with the wrist, and the main impact should be with the first and second knuckles.

To get force behind a punch, soldiers will move their bodies into the hitting action. They twist forward from the waist as the arm moves, and before the arm is fully extended. The energy should come from the hips and waist, not just the shoulders. Troops do not expect to win a fight with the first punch—even an experienced boxer does not try for that. Elite soldiers will use the first punch or two to distract an opponent; they will open him up by making him block his attacks before stepping in with one or two finishing strikes.

The chop

The side of the hand can also be used to hit an opponent, especially against soft areas, such as the throat. This is also a good way to attack joints such as the inside of the elbow, and this helps to loosen an attacker's grip. The soldier keeps the fingers straight and hits with the fleshy edge between the wrist and the base of the fingers.

Elbows

Elbows are hard, bony, and pointed. They make excellent weapons at close range, delivering a surprising amount of power without requiring a great degree of skill.

Fingers form a very effective weapon for elite troops.

Legs

Legs have some of the most powerful muscles in a person's body, and the bony knee can deliver incredibly effective strikes at close range. If a soldier is comparatively light or small, he or she can still deliver a powerful blow without too much effort. By driving the knee into the side of a person's thigh, a soldier can give someone a "dead leg." It will not do any real damage, but it can temporarily paralyze the muscles, causing an opponent to fall over.

If the threat is more menacing, a soldier can use the same knee to force it hard into the groin to put the attacker out of action for longer. This lets the soldier get well clear before the attacker can even think about moving. If it does not work first time, a soldier can hold on and keep striking, and if the attacker doubles up, the soldier may grab his head and move a knee into the enemy's face.

Here, a soldier draws his opponent toward him before driving the knee into the groin of his opponent, which will disable him for a short time.

Feet

The main kick used by the elite troops is the sidekick. If soldiers turn side-on to an opponent, they can thrust out with the sole of the foot. Troops are trained to keep the kick low, preferably at their attacker's knees. The advantage of this kick is that soldiers do not lose their balance if they miss.

If an attacker is standing very close to the soldier, short stamping kicks to his knees, legs, ankles, or feet can be useful. If the attacker is facing him, the soldier can stamp down onto his knee. This can damage his kneecap, and even if the soldier misses, his foot will rake down the attacker's shin toward the instep. If the soldier is side-on to the attacker, a sideways stamp to the knee has a chance of breaking the knee joint.

Although soldiers are taught to kick low, preferably at knee height, a high kick in the stomach can inflict immense pain on an opponent.

The head is one of the most vulnerable areas of the body, so you must do everything to protect it. This elite soldier forces his left arm in a defensive position to stop a club attack to his head.

TARGET AREAS OF THE BODY

Successful self-defense is as much about being able to strike the right target as it is about being able to perform the actual moves. Knowledge of an attacker's vulnerable spots is essential if soldiers are to achieve their aim but these skills must only be used in a truly life-threatening situation.

If a soldier gets into a fight or is attacked, he or she needs to have a target in mind for each blow or grab. Soldiers are therefore taught where the weak spots are on an opponent's body.

The head

Where the head goes, so does the rest of the body. Elite soldiers put someone on the ground by pushing their opponent's chin back and then turning his head. If he braces his neck, soldiers will push back first with a palm strike to the chin, then turn his head to one side. They can combine this with jabs to the eyes or strikes under the nose before he goes down.

The eyes

The head also holds other vulnerable targets. The eyes are probably the most obvious. A finger jabbed into them or a comb raked across sideways will cause extreme pain. If soldiers are grabbed, they can even run their hands up their attacker's face until their fingers find their opponent's eyes and then just jab them in. A successful attack will cause extreme pain, while the assailant's tear ducts will produce

In this case, the soldier raises both arms across his face to prevent the blow from reaching its target.

so much water that it will make it nearly impossible for him to see clearly. Jabs to the eyes are also good for opening up an opponent to further attacks. Even if the soldier's strike fails to make proper contact, the opponent's reflex will be to shut his eyes tightly and to try to defend with his hands. He is now wide open for another attack, whether to the head, **torso**, or legs.

The nose
The base of the nose and the upper lip have a large number of nerve endings, and can be very painful if pushed or struck. Soldiers can

also use the nose as a lever, by driving their fingers into their opponent's nostrils and pulling or pushing up. If someone is trying to bite, soldiers will not pull back, as that just helps the opponent cause damage. Instead, elite soldiers will push into their attacker's mouth, while at the same time driving the fingers or thumbs into their opponent's cheek. This pushes the flesh into his own teeth, making it impossible for him to bite down hard.

A word of warning: Soldiers can easily cause severe or even fatal damage by attacking the head in the wrong way. Troops never club down on the top of the head of an attacker, especially with a weapon, unless their aim is to kill their opponent. Similar warnings apply to the neck and throat. Troops attack the throat or side of the neck only if their lives are in danger, since this could cause the person to become **unconscious** or die.

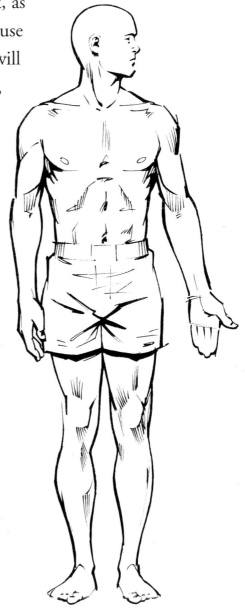

The head, particularly the eyes, and the groin are the main target areas and will incapacitate a person.

The torso

The central torso is fairly strong, although this depends to some extent on the level of fitness of the attacker. A knee into the stomach can sometimes wind someone, but troops do not rely on this. The kidneys are relatively unprotected to the rear, and a blow here can cause extreme pain.

The groin

This is extremely vulnerable. A knee, a kick, a punch, or a strike from the side of a hand can all cause great pain. And if an elite soldier is being held in close, a tight grab can disable the opponent.

If a soldier cannot get up from the ground, he must fight back hard by aiming blows at the attacker's vital areas. The groin is a good target.

The shins and knees are also excellent targets when fighting from the ground. By lying on his side, the soldier is able to use his arms and legs for support.

Arms

If soldiers have sticks or clubs, they can strike the wrist, the top of the forearm, or the inside of the upper arm muscle. A good hit in any of these places will cause pain and may deaden the limb, or even break the wrist joint. None of these are likely to be permanently harmful, but it will let a soldier escape an attack.

Hands

Hands are an obvious target in a fight. For example, the fingers can all be bent back, and this will cause great pain with comparatively little effort. A soldier can also grab one finger of the attacker in each hand and pull them wide apart for a similar effect.

If attacked by someone with a knife, the soldier can either kick at his assailant's knee or block the thrust of the knife, draw his opponent in, and execute a powerful knee to the stomach.

Legs

The knees are also extremely vulnerable, especially on larger, heavy individuals. Soldiers can stamp down on the front of the kneecap and disconnect it. If they miss, they can slide the foot all the way down the shin and press it on to the attacker's foot. A similar stamping attack to the side of the knee can also break it, while stamping into the back of the knee will fold the leg, usually dropping the attacker on the ground.

Another target on the legs is the "dead leg" area, the nerve point in the side of the thigh, halfway between the hip and knee. The value of this attack, or hitting the nerve points on the arm, is that it will work no matter how motivated the attacker is.

Feet

Soldiers can stamp down on an attacker's foot. If they put their full weight onto someone's foot, it can trap him. From here, a firm push will cause their attacker to lose his balance and fall to the ground. This gives soldiers time to either finish him off or get away.

Using everyday items as weapons

Whatever training elite soldiers may have had, many combat situations, especially in an urban environment will be unexpected. The mood of a previously calm crowd can change suddenly, and without warning, the soldiers may be required to take action.

If the soldiers are unarmed, they may need to use everyday items such as newspapers and spray cans to defend themselves.

Dropping his body to achieve maximum leverage, this U.S. soldier throws a comrade over his hip.

These can be potential lifesavers in a self-defense situation, giving soldiers extra aids with which to fend off an attacker.

The "Kubotan"

This is a short bar, some six inches (15 cm) long and a half inch (1 cm) in diameter, made from hard plastic or aluminum, with large ribs and a rounded tapered point at one end. It usually has a hole at the other end, letting it hold a soldier's keys. This can be used in various ways to inflict pain on an attacker, without being very dangerous. If an elite soldier does not have a Kubotan, any hard bar shape, such as a ballpoint pen, can make a useful substitute.

If someone grabs an elite soldier, he or she can lie the Kubotan across the nerve at the top of the wrist. The soldier will hold both ends of the Kubotan, then roll it downward and into the assailant's chest. This will inflict pain on the wrist and should cause the attacker to drop down into a crouch. The soldier can then drive a knee into the attacker's face before escaping. By pushing the Kubotan between the opponent's fingers and squeezing them tightly together, the elite soldier will also cause a fair amount of pain.

The Kubotan can also be used as a jabbing weapon by driving it into soft areas on the attacker's body. If the opponent is facing the elite soldier and coming toward him, the soldier can drive the Kubotan into the soft area of the neck below the Adam's apple and above the "v" made by the **clavicle** bones. He will push hard, which will make an attacker step back and let go of him. If he has a tight hold, such as a bear hug, from the front, the soldier holds it

horizontally, with one hand on either end, and drives it side-on, hard up into the base of his attacker's nose, pushing his head up and back until he lets go. Another target is in the soft area under the jaw, directly in line with the ear. He will swing the pen or Kubotan around the side and drive it hard up under the jaw. This is useful if an attacker is side-on to him.

If a soldier is attacked by a knife-wielding opponent, he should remain calm and wait for the opportunity to strike.

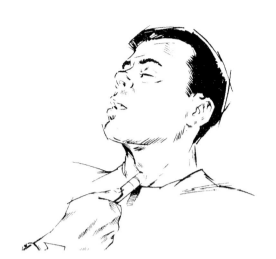 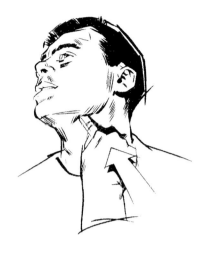

The Kubotan is an effective tool if used correctly. It can be forced into an attacker's neck (left) or hard up under the jaw (right).

If the attacker is further away, an alternative target is the soft area on the shoulder. Jabbing the Kubotan into the gap between the collarbone and the shoulder join can often force an attacker to drop that arm back away from a soldier. If nothing else, he can grip the Kubotan in his hand to make a punch heavier, more effective, and safer for his hands. Any other small heavy object can help here.

Miscellaneous items

An off-duty soldier may also have access to deodorant sprays, combs, and newspapers. Sprays, for example, are a useful defense against dangerous dogs. A comb, especially if it is metal, can be raked across someone's face, while something like a plastic credit card can be wedged up under the nose. A magazine or newspaper, if rolled up tightly, can be driven into an attacker's stomach or **solar plexus**, or be jabbed into vulnerable areas like the throat.

GLOSSARY

Adrenaline Also called epinephrine, this is a chemical released into the body by the adrenal glands. Adrenaline is the body's defense mechanism to pain and/or fear.

Adrenal glands A pair of organs situated near the kidneys, which produce adrenaline.

Adversary An opponent. A person who resists; the enemy.

Anarchist Someone who doesn't believe in government or laws.

Antagonize To irritate; to annoy.

Assertive To be assertive is to have confidence and show others you have a determination to succeed.

Captivity Confinement, often in prisons. During wartime, prisoners of war (POWs) are held in captivity.

Clavicle Another word for the collarbone, which is situated between the neck and the shoulder.

Defuse To make less harmful, potent, or intense. Usually used in the context of "defusing" a situation.

Exhale To breathe out air.

Feign To pretend; to give a false impression.

Gestures The motions of your hands and arms to express an opinion, without talking.

Horizontal To do something in a parallel manner, level with the ground.

Immobile To be out of action. If someone is immobilized, he or she may be unable to walk or talk, for instance.

Indiscriminate To be haphazard or random. If a soldier fires his gun indiscriminately, it means he fires in a variety of directions, perhaps at nothing in particular.

Interrogation To be questioned and probed for information, usually in a military sense. During wartime, POWs are interrogated by their captors to make them reveal secret information.

Intimidate To make someone frightened or fearful.

Lethal Deadly. A lethal gunshot wound, for instance, is one that causes death.

Macho Someone who exhibits machismo; a strong sense of masculine (male) pride.

Martial arts Ancient Asian fighting techniques —such as karate, kung fu, and tae kwon do.

Paralyze To render someone unable to move or speak. There are varying degrees of paralysis and it can be a temporary or permanent condition.

Posture The position of a person's body, whether relaxed or aggressive.

SAS The Special Air Service. An elite unit with the British Army, famed for covert (secret) missions and hostage rescue.

Self-defense The technique of defending yourself from an aggressor.

Solar plexus A nerve plexus in the abdomen, situated behind the stomach and the diaphragm. To be hit in this area is extremely painful.

Suppress To put down by authority or force.

Temples The flattened space on each side of the forehead of some mammals, including humans.

Torso The area between the stomach and neck of the human body.

Violate To do harm to a person or fail to show them respect.

FURTHER INFORMATION

Special Forces soldiers are sent all over the world on a variety of dangerous missions. Because they encounter all manner of hostile enemy forces, it is important that they are trained to defend themselves from all methods of attack. They are taught self-defense techniques and unarmed combat so they know what to do to overcome the enemy in situations when they do not have a weapon.

Some of the world's military forces, and the combat techniques they employ, are listed below:

Spetsnaz
- Unarmed combat with an emphasis on lethal strikes. They have their own code of practice, known as Russian Martial Arts (RMA).

Swiss Army
- They specialize in unarmed grappling techniques, including fighting from the floor and grappling on the floor.

British Paratroops
- Soldiers training to join the British Parachute Regiment practice "milling." This is an exercise that involves standing toe-to-toe with a fellow recruit and exchanging punches for a full minute. Although milling resembles boxing, it is not, because the soldier is not allowed to duck or weave. He must take all the punishment his opponent dishes out.

Egyptian Army Rangers
- Use locks and constrictions to disarm and overcome their enemies.

Japanese Army
- Japanese soldiers use traditional martial arts like karate and kung fu.

South Korean Army
- They use tae kwon do, a martial art similar in many respects to karate.

FURTHER READING

Benson, Ragnar. *Ragnar's Urban Survival*. Boulder, Colo.: Paladin Press, 2000.

Cartmell, Tim and Crandall, Ron. *Principles, Analysis, and Application of Effortless Combat Throws*. Burbank, Ca.: Unique Publications, 1998.

Franco, Sammy. *Killer Instinct: Unarmed Combat for Street Survival*. Boulder, Colo.: Paladin Press, 1991.

MacYoung, Marc. *Taking it to the Street: Making Your Martial Arts Street Effective*. Boulder, Colo.: Paladin Press, 1999.

Mizhou, Md Hui. *Effective Techniques for Unarmed Combat*. Burbank, Ca.: Unique Publications, 2000.

Perkins, John (ed). *Attack Proof: The Ultimate Guide to Personal Protection*. Champaign, Ill.: Human Kinetics, 2000.

Vancook, Jerry. *Real World Self Defense: A Guide to Staying Alive in Dangerous Times*. Boulder, Colo.: Paladin Press, 1999.

ABOUT THE AUTHOR

Patrick Wilson was educated at Marlborough College, Wiltshire and studied history at Manchester University. He was a member of the Officer Training Corps, and for the past seven years he has been heavily involved in training young people in the art of survival on CCF and Duke of Edinburgh Courses. He has taught history at St. Edward's School, Oxford, Millfield School, and currently at Bradfield College in England.

His main passion is military history. His first book was *Dunkirk—From Disaster to Deliverance* (Pen & Sword, 2000). Since then he has written *The War Behind the Wire* (Pen & Sword, 2000), which accompanied a television documentary on prisoners of war. He recently edited the diaries of an Australian teenager in the First World War.

INDEX

References in italics refer to illustrations